52

5-minute

SERMONS

for kids

Anne Pilmoor

Copyright © 2018, Autumn House Publications (Europe) Ltd.

Published in 2018 by Autumn House Publications (Europe) Ltd, Grantham, Lincolnshire, UK.

British Library Cataloguing in Publication Data. A catalogue record for this book is available from the British Library.

ISBN 978-1-78665-977-4

Designed by Abigail Murphy.
Printed in Serbia.

CONTENTS

24 We grow when we are positive and turn obstacles into opportunities.

25 Each one of us is given special talents we must use.

26 There are many pathways in life that do not end in happiness. The only path that leads to happiness is the one where Jesus takes the lead and walks beside us.

27 We can spread happiness wherever we are.

28 God uses us to spread His good news.

29 Talents are to be used and developed: not hidden.

30 Don't judge!

31 A positive attitude brings good health.

32 God should be our only treasure.

33 Understand the difference between a life filled with the Spirit and one that is not.

34 Jesus is the 'water of life'.

35 Prayer is like oxygen to the Christian.

36 Be slow to anger.

37 Don't be deceived!

38 We reap what we sow.

39 Don't be trapped by sin.

40 Don't gossip!

41 Magnify God in your life!

42 God protects me in the storms.

43 Hard hearts aren't as good as soft hearts.

44 Teamwork and encouragement go together.

45 Whatever is inside spills out when you are squeezed.

46 God protects me and saves me.

47 Open the heart to God.

48 Are you who you say you are, or are you a pretend Christian?

49 We can have forgiveness and a fresh start.

50 Half the battle is won with a positive attitude.

51 The more you give away God's love, the more you receive – it never runs out!

52 Make some new year's promises to God.

INTRODUCTION

It is hoped that this book of 52 5-minute sermons for kids will be a helpful resource, not only in the church, but also in the home. A year's supply of short illustrated sermons may be just the life-saver you need when the creative juices run dry! Each story draws on a Bible verse, and contains an object lesson with mostly readily available resources you will find in your home and garage or garden shed. You may need to gather resources a day in advance for one or two sermons, but they are still easy to assemble.

Some sermons combine a story and practical object lesson, while others simply develop spiritual thinking through the object lesson alone. Where stories and illustrations intertwine, the illustrations are nestled in square brackets [ ] for simplicity's sake.

Use these sermons with all the flexibility and creativity you obviously possess. The stories in this book may spark better stories in your toolbag – just mix and match these with yours to suit the children who will listen, learn and grow.

Acknowledgements

1. I would like to thank the Reverend Donald McCorkindale for his kind permission to use '4 Corners of God's Love' in Sermon 51, originally sent to his website *www.talks2children.wordpress.com* by Ken Forbes.

2. My grateful thanks to Roger Darlington at *www.rogerdarlington.me.uk* for permission to adapt the following stories:
   - The Story of the Pencil in Sermon 7
   - The Seven Wonders of the World in Sermon 12
   - New Glasses in Sermon 20
   - A Boulder in the Path in Sermon 24

Anne Pilmoor

sermon ①

THEME

We stay connected to God when we pray.

BIBLE GEM

'Draw near to God and He will draw near to you.'
James 4:8 (NKJV)

YOU WILL NEED

- Torch/flashlight
- A small piece of paper inserted next to the battery beforehand to break the circuit (make sure the battery works, and have a spare, just in case!)

ILLUSTRATION

Oh dear! One evening this week, we tried to make a cake for the guests we had invited for lunch the following day. We followed the recipe exactly [elaborate on the ingredients that will make children drool!] and everything seemed perfect when, all of a sudden, the electricity went off. At first, we panicked. What were we going to do about the cake that had just gone into the oven? We couldn't serve our guests raw cake, could we?

Then I remembered: 'First, check the electricity box and see whether any of the switches have tripped!' But there was another problem to deal with: it was dark, and we couldn't see anything in the electricity box. It seemed the problems were piling up fast.

'Quick! A torch . . . get me a torch!' I shouted to everyone in the house. I heard scrambling and finally [name] brought the torch. I pushed down the switch like this. [Show them.]

'Uh-oh! Did you see the bulb light up?'

6

'No!' I didn't either. ['Better push harder!'] That didn't work.

All this time the oven was cooling down, and all I could think of was a flat, horrible gooey splodge that would end up in the bin.

I scratched my head, pacing up and down the kitchen trying to figure out what might be wrong with the torch [you could get children to make suggestions]. Eventually, I opened it to check if it needed a battery [open the torch]. And this is what I found! [Show them a tiny piece of paper.] I found a little piece of paper stuck between the battery and the connector strip. Paper is not a good conductor of electricity and it had broken the circuit. The energy from the battery couldn't get through to the bulb because of the paper. The bulb could never light up with it there. I put the battery back in [like this], without the piece of paper. I pushed the button to switch it on [like this] and 'there was light'!

And it reminded me that we are like torches, too. When we don't bother or forget to pray, it is like the paper between the battery and the connector strip that stops it from working properly. Our 'lights' can't shine. Pride, disappointment, anger and selfishness can all be like those little pieces of paper that stop the energy from the battery reaching the light bulb. This week, be sure to keep your torches working well. Stay connected to God. Don't let anything break the circuit. 'Draw near to God and He will draw near to you.'

PRAYER

Dear Father, God, I want to be connected to You always; to shine Your light. . . . Remove anything from my life that breaks the circuit. Amen.

sermon ②

THEME

It is good to say sorry and make things right when we have done wrong.

BIBLE GEM

'Confess your sins to one another and pray for one another, so that you may be healed.'
James 5:16 (CSB)

YOU WILL NEED

Some knitting with dropped stitches that have left big holes (if you are not a knitter, you can pick up a cardigan or jumper at a charity shop and unravel it so that you can pick up a row of stitches halfway up, or simply make some large holes in an old jumper you no longer use)

ILLUSTRATION

[Name] is a very good friend of mine [tell the children a little about this friend and some of the reasons why he/she is so special to you].

A few weeks ago I decided to make a jumper for my friend's birthday, which is a few months away. The problem is that I dropped some stitches when I remembered the times I hadn't been the greatest friend to him/her. [You can show a hole and give an example for one or two times you have let the friend down. . . .]

[Hold up the knitting, and ask the children if it will look good enough to wear with the holes.] Are they obvious? Do you think my friend would be impressed with it and do you think he/she would wear it? Should I leave the holes? If I want to get rid of the holes, how can I fix it? I may need to undo the rows to the first hole and pick up from there.

I decided that saying sorry to my friend and making things right would be like undoing those rows with the mistakes. I would do it because our friendship is important to me and I value my friend.

Jesus is my best friend. He is important to me and I value Him as my friend, too. If I were knitting Him a jumper, there would have been holes in that one as well! In prayer, I will say sorry for the way I have let Him down.

Do you know of anyone you should say sorry to and make things right with? Why not do it today? Go on, let's knit beautiful jumpers without any holes in them!

PRAYER

Dear Jesus, I have upset some of my family and friends. Help me to tell them how much I love them and why I want to make things right. Give me the courage to say sorry to them. Amen.

sermon ③

THEME

We must guard against the pressures and influences around us or they will spoil the plans Jesus has for us.

BIBLE GEM

'Other seed fell among thorns, which grew up and choked the plants.' *Matthew 13:7 (NIV)*

YOU WILL NEED

Some bindweed from the garden or another rampant climbing plant (even better if you can show an example of one choking a flower or stem of another plant)

ILLUSTRATION

I like beautiful gardens. I like gardening. It is hard work, digging, pruning, planting, mowing, watering and weeding. I like planting best and I really dislike weeding. You see, I have a problem with bindweed [show them]. The more I try to get rid of it, the worse it gets and the more it grows!

At the end of last summer, I promised myself that I would get on top of the bindweed as soon as the new shoots started to appear in the spring. I wasn't going to have any bindweed wrapping itself around any of my roses, my hydrangeas and shrubs. I had a 'perfect plan'. (Those were famous last words.) I was so busy in the early spring, I only had time enough to take a quick look at the garden in the early morning to notice the bindweed poking its first shoots through the ground. 'Still time to deal with it,' I bluffed myself! The weeks went by and I didn't get on top of it. I tried pulling the spiralling stems away from my roses

– look, it pulled the stems and flowers away with it. The flowers and leaves were torn off and stripped. [Show the children.]

As I pulled away the menacing strands of bindweed that were choking the life out of my healthy plants, it reminded me how similar it is with our lives. Jesus used weeds as an example in the parable of the sower. He said they 'grew up and choked the plants'.

There are all kinds of distractions, influences and pressures that are just like that bindweed [get the children to suggest some examples]. Before we know it, we forget to connect with God in prayer, we don't take time to read our Bibles, or, if we do, we don't think enough about what God tells us, to allow His words to take root in our hearts. Soon, we find that we are not living the way He has shown us how to live and we don't grow to be like Jesus.

I made excuses for not dealing with the problem when the bindweed was just beginning to send out shoots. If I had pulled them out straight away, they may not have been such a problem for my plants. When we notice our habits or other influences spoiling us, it is good to take action right away so they don't take over our lives and change us. . . . Jesus has promised to help us when we ask.

Your life is like a beautiful garden. Look after it well, enjoy reading your Bible . . . and pray often. . . . Like fragrant flowers, spread your goodness to those around you. Control the weeds; get rid of them as soon as they appear, so your life will be like a healthy, well-cared-for garden that will grow and thrive. . . .

PRAYER

Dear Jesus, my life is like a garden. Help me to look after it well, to feed and water it regularly and to make sure the weeds do not spoil the plants. Amen.

sermon ④

THEME

It is good to listen to my parents' advice and instruction.

BIBLE GEM

'My child, listen when your father corrects you. Don't neglect your mother's instruction.'
Proverbs 1:8 (NLT)

YOU WILL NEED

- A picture – cover it over completely with four or five pieces of light card (make sure it is a picture that will make the children guess five different subjects as parts of it are exposed, and with a total surprise when the picture is fully exposed)
- Four or five pieces of paper to cover the picture; number them so that you will know the sequence to pull them off in
- Blu-Tack to stick pieces of paper onto the picture

ILLUSTRATION

I found a great picture recently that I like very much. It is covered, though. I wonder if you can guess what it is about? [Give a few children opportunity to guess. Then ask one child to lift off the card numbered 1. It will expose only a small part of the picture and should be hard to make out. Ask them if they have a better idea what the picture is about now. Get them to give another few guesses. Move on to the card numbered 2 and continue this way until the entire picture is revealed.]

That was interesting. We thought we knew what the picture was about, only to find out that it was something different when all the pieces of paper were removed and we could see the whole picture. When I was your age, I started to be a bit of a 'know-all'. I wasn't always good at following the advice of my parents. When they cautioned me not to do certain things, or to be careful about the influence of certain individuals, I thought they were fuddy-duddy and just wanted to spoil my fun [give some examples of your own]. It was just like the picture that was completely covered by the card. I couldn't see what they could see. I couldn't understand what they understood.

As time went on and I started to understand better that I didn't know as much as I thought I did, I realised that my parents had seen more and experienced more of life. They knew what they were talking about. They knew the dangers; they also knew about the opportunities that were for the taking if I was sensible. They weren't spoiling my fun at all; they were trying to help me enjoy life even more and make the most of the best opportunities it had to offer. You see, they could see the bigger picture all along! I couldn't!

The wise man in the Bible says, 'My child, listen when your father corrects you. Don't neglect your mother's instruction.' Wise children take note of their parents' advice because they know their parents can see the bigger picture. Be wise!

PRAYER

Dear Jesus, thank You for my parents. You chose the right ones for me! Help me to show them respect and to follow their advice. Amen.

sermon 5

THEME

Selfless people make time and place in their lives to help others.

BIBLE GEM

'When you do things, do not let selfishness or pride be your guide. Instead, be humble . . .'
Philippians 2:3-4 (NCV)

YOU WILL NEED

- A narcissus or daffodil (real or artificial)
- A small vase
- A few small flowers

ILLUSTRATION

Can anyone tell me the name of this flower? Some call it a daffodil. It is really part of the narcissus family. Narcissus is a Greek word often linked to the mythical young man of that name who fell in love with his own reflection.

It is said that the narcissus cannot bear competition with other flowers in a vase because it draws attention to itself. It is too proud! [Arrange the flowers quickly in the vase to illustrate the point.] It is true: they do not arrange well with other flowers and are best displayed on their own or with other narcissi.

To this day, we call someone who is so wrapped up in themselves, who has no empathy or sensitivity for others, a narcissist.

Jesus was quite the opposite. He never put His own interests above the needs of others.

The apostle Paul commented on Jesus' example and teaching, and told us to choose humility above pride and to put others' needs and interests before our own.

Why not follow that advice this week? If you were a flower, what would you be, and could you be part of a beautiful arrangement in a vase with lots of different flowers?

PRAYER

Dear Jesus, I want a pure heart. . . . I want to make others happy for the right reasons, not just because I want to look good in the eyes of everyone else! Give me pure motives in all I do. Amen.

sermon 6

THEME

Live and work in harmony with others.

BIBLE GEM

'Live in peace with each other. Do not be proud, but make friends with those who seem unimportant. Do not think how smart you are.'
Romans 12:16 (NCV)

YOU WILL NEED

- Either get the pianist to play a tune and have the children sing a different song (for example, play 'Twinkle, twinkle, little star' and have the children sing 'Jesus loves me');

Or

- Get three singers to each sing a different song at the same time;

Or

- Get three instrumentalists to each play a different song at the same time
  (it must sound dreadful!)

ILLUSTRATION

I like to sing. Do you? I thought it would be great if we could sing together now . . . will you join me? [Tell the children which song they will sing and don't tell them that the accompaniment will be an entirely different tune. The accompaniment must be very loud so that it will put the children off.]

As soon as the singing appears to be a mess, get the children and the accompanist/s to stop. Ask the children what went wrong? Did they not know the song? Ask them to try again. Stop them again when it is obviously falling apart. Tell them you were expecting the singing to be harmonious. It wasn't. It was jarring. The people in the congregation were covering their ears, it was so bad!

The Bible is filled with calls for us to live in harmony with one another. It also gives lots of examples of sad consequences for those who thought they were better than others, or hurt others, or took things that did not belong to them. When Jesus came to our world, He showed us what an unselfish person looks like; how to be at peace with everyone, and how to live in harmony with one another.

[Talk about what it means to live in harmony. Some of the principles you could touch on are agreeing to live by the same rules: for example, the Ten Commandments, the golden rule, working together for an agreed outcome for the better good of all.]

[Finally, sing and play one song beautifully and get some good singers to add to the harmony.]

Wasn't that beautiful? When we live and work in harmony that is how beautiful life can be. . . .

What will you do to make the coming week a harmonious one?

PRAYER

Gracious Jesus, help me always to live in harmony with You and to fill the air with singing! Amen.

sermon

THEME

God has a special purpose for everyone.

BIBLE GEM

'And we know that in all things God works for the good of those who love him, who have been called according to his purpose.' *Romans 8:28 (NIV)*

YOU WILL NEED

- A box of pencils
- A collection of different writing/drawing implements (for example, pens, felt-tip pens, crayons, chalks or pastels)

ILLUSTRATION

Today I brought a collection of things we use to either write or draw [show the children]: pens, pencils, felt-tip pens, crayons and chalks. I've used them all, but each kind for very specific things. This week I used the pen to write a birthday card. I used the pencil to answer a questionnaire, so I could rub out an answer, if I changed my mind. I helped my little niece colour a picture using these crayons and I used the felt-tip pen to label a parcel. My friend drew a beautiful picture with the pastels. These objects all make marks. The neat thing about them is that they only work when someone holds them and uses them. Another special feature about them is that the pencils cannot do what crayons do, and the marks made with felt-tips cannot be rubbed out like pencil marks can. Each of them has a different purpose.

Imagine if I used the chalks to label a parcel! The mark would soon rub off and the parcel would be lost! Imagine if I tried to colour my niece's picture with a black ink pen! That would be a mess!

Our verse tells us that God made us to do something very special for Him. He may have created you to be like a pencil and your friend to be like a crayon: both are similar, but different, and no one better than the other. He created both for a particular purpose.

I once read a story about an old pencil maker who took the last pencil he had made aside before putting it in the pencil box. He started talking to the pencil as if it were his son!

'There are five things you must know before I send you out into the world. Never forget these five things and you will be sure to be the best pencil you can be!' the pencil maker said.

'Remember first, you have the ability to do many great things, but only if you put yourself in someone else's hands;

'Second, from time to time you will have the pain of someone putting you through a sharpener – remember, this will only make you a better pencil;

'Third, remember that you are a pencil, and any mistake you make can be erased and corrected;

'Fourth, the most important part of you is what is on the inside;

'And finally remember, whatever you are expected to write on, to leave a good mark. You were made for writing. Write well!'

You know, the good advice to the pencil is good for each one of us!

PRAYER

Dear Jesus, it is exciting to know You made me to do something special and wonderful for You. Help me to be a good pencil that writes well. Amen.

sermon (8)

THEME
Although small, my influence spreads far and wide.

BIBLE GEM
'Then Jesus told another story: "The kingdom of heaven is like yeast that a woman took and hid in a large tub of flour until it made all the dough rise." ' *Matthew 13:33 (NCV)*

YOU WILL NEED
- Either a small lump of live yeast or a little sachet of dried yeast
- A dough mix made with yeast that has risen
- A dough mix made without any raising agent
- A fresh loaf of bread

ILLUSTRATION

Jesus told the story about the yeast that causes the dough to double its size. [Show the sachet and talk about how just a teaspoon of it was able to make the dough rise. Show the other example of dough without any raising agent – what a difference the yeast made to the dough.]

Jesus explained that the small things make a big difference, and that our influence, though seemingly insignificant, is the same. We may feel that only the rich, the famous and the powerful can make a difference, but that isn't true.

Recently I heard about a lady who felt so small, so unimportant and helpless. She had overcome some challenges in her life and wanted to make other people feel important and loved. She started leaving encouraging little notes on the bus seats, in the train, on the shop counters, on notice boards, in shopping trolleys – anywhere someone might pick one up. People started to talk about the notes and how special they had made them feel. Someone reported it on the radio, then the television. No one knew who was writing these special notes for them, but they seemed to have just the right message for the right person at the right time. Encouraged, the letter-writer aimed to write a million letters to people who were lonely or discouraged and wanted to receive a special letter. On the web she encouraged people to let her know. She is still writing letters to people all over the world, and what a difference she has made.

Your special gift may be a beautiful smile or a polite gesture that will make someone's day – whatever it is, just like the yeast, you can make a lump of dough turn into something wonderful! Go on, give it a try!

PRAYER

Dear Jesus, thank You for sharing Your story about yeast and helping me to understand that small things matter and make a huge difference. Help me to be like yeast that always makes a beautiful loaf. Amen.

sermon 9

THEME

Our choices have lasting consequences for good or bad.

BIBLE GEM

'As for me and my family, we will serve the LORD.'
Joshua 24:15 (NCV)

YOU WILL NEED

A piece of wood, a hammer and nails

ILLUSTRATION

God shows us the right path to take in our lives, but He doesn't force us to take that path. He wants us to make choices for ourselves.

[Explain that our choices can sometimes have lasting consequences.] Randy started on a good path, but he got discouraged because some of his friends at church weren't kind to him. He should have sorted it out by talking to them and explaining how they made him feel, but he didn't. [Hammer in a nail for each unfortunate choice and consequence.]

First he blamed God . . .

Then he stopped reading his Bible . . .

Then he stopped praying . . .

He stopped going to his Bible study group . . .

He stopped going to church . . .

He made friends with a rough crowd . . .

They persuaded him it was cool to try drinking and they hung around the park, drinking . . .

They started vandalising the play equipment . . .

One day the police caught them red-handed and marched them to the police station.

They were charged for damaging public property and he was given a criminal record.

His life spiralled further and further into disaster and misery [hammer in some more nails].

He was sent to a young offenders' detention centre where he learned even more bad things, like how to rob a bank;

How to steal a car;

How to copy someone's bank card . . .

But a kind pastor visited the centre. He looked for the kernel of goodness still left in the young man's heart and he told him all the wonderful experiences he could have if he left his bad choices behind and had a fresh start [start removing the nails]. The young man hugged the pastor and asked him to help him. He thanked him for showing him a better way. He started to change his ways. Before long the wardens felt it was safe to let him go home, on the understanding that the pastor kept a close eye on him.

Randy repented of his ways and the nails were removed, but the holes remained [show the holes]. Despite a changed life, the scars remained. Even when we change, we sometimes have to live with the scars of our bad choices.

Sometimes people make wrong choices because they are deceived, like Randy, but other times it is just due to their wilful selfishness.

Determine to serve Jesus today and every day. Let Him guide you to make choices that have good and lasting consequences for you and all who are in your family and circle of friends.

PRAYER

Dear Father, God, thank You for giving me choices and for not forcing me to do anything against my will – help me to respect that by being responsible, by making the best choices; I want to be like You, bringing happiness to my family and friends. Amen.

sermon (10)

THEME

Christians are called to share each other's burdens.

BIBLE GEM

'By helping each other with your troubles, you truly obey the law of Christ.' *Galatians 6:2 (NCV)*

YOU WILL NEED

- A large, clear glass filled three-quarters of the way up with water
- A large, clear glass filled with a very strong salt solution
- Two eggs

ILLUSTRATION

Jim and Peter were great friends. They did everything together. Sometimes they even went on holiday together. They were like brothers!

One day Jim noticed that Peter didn't seem his happy, normal self. No one else would have noticed it, but Jim knew him so well, he could tell something wasn't right. He asked Peter if something was bothering him, but Peter just shook his head and said, 'Nah! Everything's fine. Maybe I just look tired because I sat up half the night finishing the History project.'

A few weeks later Peter seemed to be quieter still. He didn't finish his packed lunch as he normally did. He didn't want to join in the football game anymore, either. Now it was obvious to *everyone* that something wasn't right with Peter.

One morning his teacher did a little experiment for class worship.

She told them that Jesus told us that we do not need to carry our burdens on our own. As Christians we should help one another and bear one another's burdens. She told them to think of someone they knew very well. 'Think of some of the burdens they have, things that are troubling them, and imagine they are weighing them down – just like this egg [slip the egg into the glass of water].' She carefully slipped the egg into the glass of water, and it gently settled to the bottom. 'But just imagine how different it could be if everyone around that person could help and ease that person's burdens?' [Slip the egg into the salt water solution.] 'It would be like putting the egg into this salt water solution. The egg is suspended and it floats towards the top. The salt in the water is supporting the egg and helping it to float.'

Jim looked at Peter and whispered, 'I know there are things that are troubling you. Shall we meet up at break to talk about it?'

Peter raised his thumbs. During the morning break, Peter shared his worries. The problems weren't solved overnight, but he felt better for sharing his worries and he felt better for knowing that Jim cared.

Jesus told His followers to be like salt – making a difference to the flavour of our food. He also told His followers to support each other until He returned, just like the salt solution that helped the egg to float. We can lighten one another's burdens when times are tough.

PRAYER

Dear Jesus, I want to help lift [name a friend]'s burdens with kind words, my warm smile and a helpful attitude. Help me to bring them happiness. Amen.

sermon (11)

THEME

We cannot fulfil His purpose for us when we exclude Jesus from our lives.

BIBLE GEM

'Our people must learn to use their lives for doing good deeds to provide what is necessary so that their lives will not be useless.' *Titus 3:14 (NCV)*

YOU WILL NEED

- A clock
- A clock battery

ILLUSTRATION

I was embarrassed several times this week. I looked at the clock and thought I had plenty of time for my appointment at the dentist – when I arrived there I discovered I was very late. Someone else was given my appointment and I had to pay a fine and arrange for a new appointment!

I was late beginning to prepare for a meal – when my visitors arrived I didn't have anything prepared! The potatoes were hard and the roast was cold. And they had to sit and wait while I panicked and struggled to rescue the situation! [Show them the clock.] All because the battery in the mantel clock had stopped working! It needed replacing. The clock was useless without a battery that worked. It's the same with us: we are like the clock, and Jesus, like the battery, gives us the energy and inspiration to do everything He expects of us. Jesus gave us instructions about living with purpose – He told us to care for the sick, to feed the hungry, to give the thirsty something to drink, to be generous to the poor. When we live only for ourselves, we are like my useless clock on the mantelpiece – in need of a new battery!

Make sure your battery is fully charged and filled with God's love!

PRAYER

Dear Jesus, fill my battery with all the energy it needs to share Your love with others. Amen.

sermon (12)

THEME

The most precious things in life cannot be bought as they are gifts from God.

BIBLE GEM

'Keep your lives free from the love of money and be content with what you have, because God has said, "Never will I leave you; never will I forsake you." ' *Hebrews 13:5 (NIV)*

YOU WILL NEED

- Downloaded photographs of: the Great Pyramids of Egypt, the Taj Mahal, the Grand Canyon, the Panama Canal, the Empire State Building, St Peter's Basilica, the Great Wall of China
- A sheet of notepaper with these words written on it: 'To see, to hear, to touch, to taste, to feel, to laugh, to love'

ILLUSTRATION

Recently, I read about a teacher who asked her class to make a list of what they considered to be the seven great wonders of the world. These were the most popular answers – maybe you can say what they are when you see the pictures [show them and possibly mention one quick interesting fact about each one].

There was one child in the class who seemed to be particularly thoughtful about the answers and she didn't complete her paper as quickly as the rest of her classmates. When her teacher asked if she needed help, she replied that she had found it difficult to list only seven, when there were so many she could choose. The teacher asked her to read out her list [read them from the notepaper]:

To see,
To hear,
To touch,
To taste,
To feel,
To laugh,
To love

The children sat in stunned silence. It is true: the things we take for granted are even greater than the most stunning buildings around the world. Paul reminds us, in our text, to be content with the gifts God has given us.

PRAYER

Dear Father God, help me to appreciate how blessed I am to be able to see, hear, touch, taste, feel, laugh and love. Thank You for these amazing gifts; they are better than the grandest palace or the fastest car. Amen.

sermon (13)

THEME

We can use God's gifts wisely, for good; or recklessly, to harm.

BIBLE GEM

'Each of you should use whatever gift you have received to serve others, as faithful stewards of God's grace. . . .' *1 Peter 4:10 (NIV)*

YOU WILL NEED

- Some builder's bricks
- A rock or two
- A trowel
- A plumb-line

ILLUSTRATION

Peter reminds us that we need to use our gifts to do good. Here are some builder's bricks and rocks and tools that builders use [show your examples]. If we had enough bricks, we could use them to build a shelter, or something even grander than that. [Talk about some of the things builders do to make sure their walls are straight, how they build the foundations to keep the building from subsiding or sinking into the ground, and how the weight-bearing walls are strengthened to keep the structure stable.] Bricks are really useful for building. . . .

Some people can do great harm with these very useful bricks, too. I have heard of people throwing them at cars and causing shocking accidents on the motorway. Some have picked them up to hurl at other people in anger or spitefulness, causing huge injury and permanent disfigurement or disability. Some have dumped used bricks and other rubble in the countryside and they have spoilt its beauty.

We are all builders, building our own characters. The habits that form our characters will determine whether we are using our gifts to build solid, useful, permanent structures, or to hurt and destroy. Today, will you choose to be a builder, not a destroyer?

PRAYER

Dear Lord, I am blessed with many gifts from You. Help me to use my 'bricks' to build something worthwhile and useful. Help me never to be tempted to use my bricks to hurt or destroy others. Amen.

sermon (14)

ILLUSTRATION

Pumice stones are quite amazing. [Show the children as you talk about their characteristics.] They are a type of lava rock that is full of bubble holes. The holes are formed as the lava shoots out of the volcano, and are then trapped as the lava cools and hardens. Pumice stones are very rough to touch, and they are often used to scrub the heels and soles of people's feet. This removes the hard, dead skin, leaving the skin soft, healthy and clean. Most people have a small pumice stone in their bathrooms. We won't be rubbing away any dead skin here today, but we can see how effective the pumice stone is by rubbing away the potato skin. [Keep rubbing the potato while you talk to the children.]

Although it doesn't really hurt, it isn't always comfortable rubbing off dead skin.

Our mistakes and bad habits are like the hard skin that the stone rubs away. [Talk about some of the bad habits that draw us away from Jesus. The potato should be fully peeled. Show the children how well it worked.] Jesus promises to be like that pumice stone, rubbing our sins away, leaving behind only that which is healthy and pure.

Think about what you would like Jesus to rub away from your life today. . . .

PRAYER

Dear Jesus, just as the pumice stone rubs away the hard skin, rub away my habits that harden me to the needs of others. Leave me pure, clean and glowing. Amen.

sermon 15

THEME

God will always keep His promises!

BIBLE GEM

'. . . You know with all your heart and soul that not one of all the good promises the LORD your God gave you has failed.' *Joshua 23:14 (NIV)*

YOU WILL NEED

- An A4 sheet of paper
- Four coloured marker pens
- Follow the instructions to make the chatterbox below or follow the demonstration on *www.kidspot.com.au*

Instructions:

Make a square from the rectangular A4 sheet by folding a right-angled triangle down from the top-right corner to the left edge, matching up the edges. Cut off the strip at the bottom, and then unfold the triangle into a square.

You should have a diagonal fold across the square; make a cross by folding the two creased corners together and opening the square again.

Fold each corner into the centre. Turn it over and fold each corner into the centre again.

Fold it in half so that the bottom and top edges of the square meet to make a rectangle. Now open it out, and then fold it again so that the left and right edges meet, and then open it out again.

Label your chatterbox with a different-coloured shape on each of the four square outer flaps. Then, on the other side, label each of the eight triangles with a number (1-8); then lift the triangular flaps and write a promise inside each of them.

ILLUSTRATION

Today we have a special chatterbox filled with some of my favourite promises from the Bible. [Put a thumb or index finger under each of the four square outer flaps, pinch them together and point them upwards, showing the children. Ask one of the children to pick a colour. Alternate between pinching the thumb and index of each hand together, and pinching your two thumbs and two index fingers together, so that it alternates opening horizontally and vertically as you spell the word of the colour. For example, if the child says 'Green', you alternate the direction on the G, then the R, then the E until you have spelt the word. Ask another child to choose a number that is displayed inside – they will have a choice of 4. Open it up and read the verse that is there. Remind the children which numbers have been taken so that you can get through all 8 promises quickly.]

[Remind the children to remember these promises when they are anxious, feel lonely or need comfort. Get them to say together, 'I will never forget that God keeps all His promises!']

PRAYER

Dear God, thank You for the many promises in the Bible I can claim when I am afraid, lonely or sad. Thank You for keeping all Your promises to me. Amen.

sermon 16

ILLUSTRATION

[Show the children the two pattern envelopes.] I wanted to make a jacket but I didn't have a pattern. My friend has loads of patterns and said I could borrow hers. I liked the style of the jacket very much. I bought the cloth and then used the pattern pieces inside to lay out on the cloth and to cut it out. But something wasn't right – there were pieces I expected to see, like the collar, for instance, but I couldn't find the pattern piece for the collar. It didn't make sense. Finally, I realised that the pattern pieces were in the wrong envelopes! . . . If I had cut out those pieces and sewn them together, I wouldn't have made a jacket at all!

Sometimes we are like those pattern pieces. The envelope says we are one thing, but the pieces inside tell what is really true! It is very easy to be a 'pretend Christian'. We say all the good things and have all the right answers, but we don't live what we preach. We don't live like Christians. We can only call ourselves Christians when our characters and lives allow the light of Jesus to shine through. Our pattern pieces (lives) match the image on the pattern envelope (Jesus). James encourages us to be honest about ourselves, to be true to ourselves. Make sure Jesus is always your Pattern!

PRAYER

Dear Jesus, be my Pattern today and every day. May every pattern piece in the envelope be the right one to fit with You and resemble You! Amen.

sermon

THEME

**We do not need to fret or worry about anything –
God is in control!**

BIBLE GEM

**'Two sparrows cost only a penny, but not even one
of them can die without your Father's knowing it.
God even knows how many hairs are on your head.
So don't be afraid. You are worth much more than
many sparrows.'** *Matthew 10:29-31 (NCV)*

YOU WILL NEED

- A fairly large suitcase
- Six very heavy objects that will fit into the case at the
  same time – each one labelled with your worries in the
  past week.

ILLUSTRATION

[Ask the children if there was anything they worried about in the
past week? Give a few children opportunities to respond. Then tell
them about your week, which was filled with all kinds of worries. Tell
them that worries can really weigh down heavily on us. Get one of the
children to pick up the suitcase before you start filling it. As you tell
them about each worry, put the heavy object with the label on it in the
suitcase. After filling the case with the sixth worry, it should be very
hard for a small child to lift. Show the difference. Tell them that you
have carried these worries around with you all week and it has been
just like that heavy case. It has been exhausting and you have had to
concentrate so hard on dragging it around, you haven't been able to
find solutions to your worries.]

When I read the text in Matthew, it reminded me that I do not need to worry, because God knows about those worries already. As I worried less, I found ways to solve the problems, or the problem turned out not to be a genuine problem after all. [As you speak of the solution to each problem, remove the worry object from the case. Finally, when it is empty, get the same child who tried to lift it when it was heavy to lift it again.] Jesus tells us we need not worry about anything. We can hand over all our worries to Him.

PRAYER

Dear Jesus, it is such a waste of time and energy to worry about all the everyday things that come my way. Help me to empty my case of worries before they weigh me down, and to hand them all to You. Thank You for giving me solutions to sort out any problems. Amen.

sermon 18

THEME

The Ten Commandments were given to us by God; they show us how to live for Him and live well with each other.

BIBLE GEM

1. You shall have no other gods before me.
2. You shall not worship idols.
3. You shall not take the name of the Lord in vain.
4. Remember the Sabbath day to keep it holy.
5. Honour your father and your mother.
6. You shall not kill.
7. You shall not commit adultery.
8. You shall not steal.
9. You shall not bear false witness.
10. You shall not covet. *Exodus 20:1-17 (simplified)*

YOU WILL NEED

Instruction manuals for an iPhone and iPad or any other devices or machinery

ILLUSTRATION

We have a file at home where we keep all the instruction manuals for our appliances, machinery and electronic devices. This week I tried to change the settings on my iPad to be the same as the settings on my iPhone. I pulled out the instructions for an iPhone [show the manuals]. I followed the instructions carefully, but some things just didn't work the way the instructions said they would! It was useless! I

40

wasted hours and hours of time, trying to do everything the manual instructed. Eventually, I made an appointment at the Apple store to get an expert to sort it out for me. Can you imagine how embarrassed I was when the expert said, 'You would have got it to work if you had used the instruction manual, mate!' I hadn't noticed that I had pulled out the manual for my son's phone, which is a different version to mine! No wonder I had such a struggle!

God has given us the best instruction manual ever to explain how to honour Him and to live with one another, but sometimes we forget to even think about those instructions. We listen to friends who don't know very much, or we are influenced by the images we see on the television, or in magazines, or books we read, and we allow them to guide us, rather than the ten perfect instructions God gave us in the Ten Commandments. Be sure to make them your instruction manual for life – you will always be blessed for following them!

PRAYER

Thank You, Father God, for giving us a perfect instruction manual to live well. Help us to remember each instruction and to live by them, always. Amen.

sermon (19)

THEME

Celebrate diversity, knowing that we are all the same in God's sight.

BIBLE GEM

'In the new life there is no difference between Greeks and Jews . . . or people who are foreigners, or Scythians. There is no difference between slaves and free people. But Christ is in all believers, and Christ is all that is important.'
Colossians 3:11 (NCV)

YOU WILL NEED

- A collection of photographs of people covering different ages, genders and ethnicities: some rich, others poor
- A small bunch of grey balloons (inflated)
- A bunch of assorted colourful balloons (inflated)

ILLUSTRATION

Today, I have brought a number of photographs of different people. [Show them as you talk about them.] This is Grandad James – he's my favourite because he is the oldest person I know [mention one remarkable interesting fact about him]. This is Julie – she's my friend and she's my favourite because she is the kindest person I know. This is Je Ahn – she's my favourite because I love music and she plays the violin beautifully. This is Sipho – he comes from Africa; he's my favourite because he tells very funny jokes that make me laugh (a lot!). This is Susan – she lives in just one tiny room and she never complains. She says she is blessed because she has a roof over her head. She's my favourite because she is content with what she has! And here is Rosemary – she lives in a mansion of a place, but she is generous to everyone. She's my favourite, too!

Our verse tells us that there is no difference between any of us, no matter how we look, where we come from, whether we are rich or poor. All that matters to the author is that Jesus lives in each one's heart!

Just imagine how boring it would be if everyone looked like me, liked everything I liked, was interested in things that only I am interested in! Life would be just like this bunch of grey balloons. I'm so glad God created our world with so much variety. It makes our world rich and interesting, just like this colourful bunch of balloons. If you had a party, which bunch would you choose? Of course, it would be the colourful bunch! That's just how God made us. Now let's go and celebrate: first, by thanking Him that we are not all the same!

PRAYER

Dear Jesus, thank You for making us all so different that there is something very special about each one of us we can enjoy and celebrate. Amen.

sermon 20

THEME

Discernment (wisdom) is a gift from God.

BIBLE GEM

'Hold on to wisdom, and it will take care of you. Love it, and it will keep you safe.' *Proverbs 4:6 (NCV)*

YOU WILL NEED

- A normal pair of glasses
- A pair of sunglasses

ILLUSTRATION

There once was a man who wore glasses just like these [normal pair of glasses – put them on]. He was a very rich man, but was at the end of his tether because he had terrible pain in the eyes. He had spent a fortune on doctor's bills to sort out the problem. He had spent a fortune on tablets and injections, but nothing seemed to make it better. It seemed to make the pain in his eyes worse than ever.

Finally, he visited a wise man, who knew a thing or two about eye problems. The wise man diagnosed the problem immediately. 'For the next few months,' he said, 'you must concentrate only on green colours. Do not look at anything that isn't green!' It seemed a very strange cure, but the rich man was so desperate, he was willing to try anything.

The rich man called in the decorators and told them to paint everything in his house green: the walls, the furniture, every object! After a few days, the wise man came to visit him to see if the cure was beginning to work. When the rich man's servants saw the wise man, they screamed in horror because he was wearing a red cloak! They dashed over to him with a bucket of green paint in their hands. They were just about to douse him in paint when . . .

'Woah,' he called out and chuckled; 'why didn't you just go out and buy a pair of green-tinted sunglasses?' [put on the green sunglasses] he asked. 'It wouldn't have cost you nearly as much in money and time. Everything in your house would have looked green when you wore them. You should have known, you cannot paint the world green!'

That is how it is with us, too: there are things in life we cannot change. We cannot change other people's behaviour or the way the world works, but we can cope with the ups and downs better if we change the way we look at the world. Real change only happens when we change ourselves.

Do you need to wear a pair of green-tinted sunglasses, perhaps? Those who are able to change their vision of the world are blessed with special wisdom that only God can give. We cannot make ourselves wise. Why not ask Him for that gift? Why not ask Him to give you better vision today?

PRAYER

Dear Jesus, what a foolish man the rich man was! We are just as foolish when we are unwilling to be changed from within. Give us wisdom and a vision of our place in the world that will really make a difference. Amen.

sermon 21

THEME

If we call ourselves Christians, we must be Christ-like.

BIBLE GEM

'Whoever says that he lives in God must live as Jesus lived.' *1 John 2:6 (NCV)*

YOU WILL NEED

- A fairly small pumpkin or squash plant in a plant pot (for ease, just get one at the garden centre)
- A plant pot with soil, with a seed that has been baked, hence no plant
- A small selection of pumpkins or squashes

ILLUSTRATION

We like pumpkins, and a few weeks ago we decided to plant some pumpkin seeds. First we planted them in pots like these [show the pots] to give them a good start. We planned to plant them in the vegetable patch a few weeks after they germinated. Pumpkins make very big plants that spread all over the ground, for very little fruit or pumpkin!

First we filled the pots with growmix, which is perfect for the seeds to germinate in. We planted the seeds about one inch deep in the soil and made sure the temperature in the greenhouse was a constant 21.1°C. This was the first seed to germinate, and within fourteen days it was pushing through a tiny shoot. We knew that if we looked after it well, we would be harvesting a pumpkin from it in about 85 days! We were excited and expected the rest of the seeds would begin to germinate. They didn't. Eventually I scratched a bit in the soil to figure out what was happening. There was nothing to see apart from a seed nestled in the soil.

'I think I know why the rest of the seeds aren't germinating,' my son volunteered. 'They can't.'

'What do you mean, they can't germinate? How do you know?'

'Remember those seeds we roasted in the oven? I put them in the potting shed thinking I was being helpful. They aren't there anymore, and I think you planted the batch of roasted seeds we were hoping to eat!'

So here we have two seeds: one growing and promising to give me a nice big pumpkin in a few months' time, and the other just a tough, hard seed that simply can't grow, even if it wanted to.

That is how it is with the fruits of the Spirit – the Bible tells us that only good seed produces the fruit of the Spirit. That fruit isn't the kind you can eat, but it is the kind that makes the world a caring place in which to live. Can anyone remember what those fruits are? [Ask them to recall them: love, joy, peace, patience, kindness, goodness, faithfulness, gentleness, self-control – those are the fruits we need to grow to be more like Jesus.] The roasted seeds that cannot grow anything, because they are hard and the life is burnt out of them, are like those who never respond to the Holy Spirit when He nudges them to develop the attributes of Jesus.

You are still young – each one of you has a seed that is healthy and strong with a potential to develop the best fruit (or pumpkin!). Take care that your seed's potential to grow never gets roasted out of it. Jesus can do so much more with a seed ready for growth.

PRAYER

I give all my seeds to You, Jesus; keep them in the best condition to germinate, grow and produce good fruit for You. Amen.

sermon 22

THEME

The Bible is God's message to us.

BIBLE GEM

'For the shepherds have become stupid and have not sought the LORD; therefore they have not prospered. . . .' *Jeremiah 10:21 (NASB)*

YOU WILL NEED

Someone to send a text message to your phone: the message must state a time to meet them at the airport on a certain date and be from an old school friend you haven't seen for many years

ILLUSTRATION

I'm still upset! Something dreadful happened this week. On Wednesday afternoon, I had a call from an old school friend. He didn't even say 'hello!' He just said, 'Where are you?' I blinked my eyes for a minute or two. 'Oh, no!' I bellowed down the phone! 'I forgot, I was supposed to meet you at the airport, wasn't I? It'll take me an hour and a half to get there! Hang in there, I'm coming,' I said, as cheerily as I could.

There was a long silence, then a long sigh from the other side. 'Sorry, I will be queuing up for my next flight by the time you get here. Don't bother!'

'That's terrible!' I wailed. 'I can't believe I didn't check my message from you. I was looking forward to catching up with you again, after all these years!'

[Look up the message on your phone and read it to them.]

'I've been patiently waiting for you since 8 o'clock this morning!' My friend sounded disappointed. 'I was so sure you'd be here to meet me when my plane landed. . . . Goodbye, my friend. I'm so sorry we never met up after all!'

My friend reminded me that Jesus has sent me important messages in the Bible, too. He has promised to meet up. . . . If I don't read His messages, I'll forget a lot of what He has told me and I'll miss out on catching up with Him. . . .

Check your messages from Jesus every day! You wouldn't want to miss out on a good old catch-up, would you?

PRAYER

Dear Jesus, let me not lose out because I haven't bothered to read Your messages to me. Remind me to check Your messages every day. Amen.

sermon  23

THEME

We all belong to Jesus.

BIBLE GEM

'My dear children, you belong to God . . . God's spirit, who is in you, is greater than the devil, who is in the world.' *1 John 4:4 (NCV)*

YOU WILL NEED

- A copy of your birth certificate, or that of someone in your family
- A cross made from wood or card

ILLUSTRATION

[Show the children your birth certificate.] This is a very important document my parents were given to prove that I was born; that I was their child; and that I have a right to be a citizen of the country where I was born.

[Show them the birth certificate. Then give them some of the information on it: mother's and father's names; their occupations; the date you were born; the address of the house they were living in at the time; all the names you were given. Tell them how they chose your names.]

This document is probably one of the most important documents I own. I have had to produce it when I went to university, when I took my driving test, when I got married, and when I was issued with my first passport. It has always provided the proof of who I am for all these important events in my life.

Here, I have another birth certificate – it's different, but even more important than the one I just showed you! [Show them the cross.] When Jesus died on the cross for me, it was the birth certificate that tells me I am entitled to live with Him in heaven. This certificate says I belong to Him and I am a citizen of His kingdom.

You have these two certificates too, just as I do! How wonderful that through Jesus' death there is eternal life for all!

PRAYER

Dear Jesus, thank You for the gift of life here with my parents, family and friends, and thank You for the promise for all of us of life forever with You! Amen.

sermon (24)

THEME

We grow when we are positive and turn obstacles into opportunities.

BIBLE GEM

'Blessed is the one who perseveres under trial because, having stood the test, that person will receive the crown of life that the Lord has promised to those who love him.' *James 1:12 (NIV)*

YOU WILL NEED

- A large rock
- A purse with coins and a hand-written note

ILLUSTRATION

A long time ago a king had a huge boulder placed on the road. He hid close to the road to see how long it would take for someone to move the boulder out of the way, and who that person might be.

He was surprised: some of the most important people in the city just walked around it! He heard people 'tut-tutting' about how useless the king was for not keeping the road in good repair. No one bothered to move the rock and clear the road – after all, it was the king's job to sort it out!

After some time a poor farmer, who was carrying a huge basket of vegetables, walked up close to the boulder. He didn't walk round it! Instead, he carefully put his vegetables on the side, used all his strength and might to push the rock out of the road, and rolled it onto the side. [Demonstrate with the rock.] As he picked up his vegetables again, he noticed a purse, which must have been under the rock before he had moved it out of the way. When he opened the purse, he found some gold coins and a note from the king which read:

'These gold coins are from the king for the person who moved the boulder out of the road. Thank you!'

That day, the poor farmer learned that obstacles are only obstacles if we keep them that way. When we see them as opportunities to make things better or improve things, what a difference it makes!

In the Bible we are reminded that there will be rocks in our path in life, too. Walking around them isn't the best way to deal with them, because the rocks will still be there! When we find a way of moving them, we improve life for ourselves and for everyone else. The Bible also tells us that when we find obstacles are put in our path because we choose to follow Jesus, we will be rewarded with a crown of life.

PRAYER

Dear Father God, give me the courage and determination to clear my path of any obstacle that stops me from making progress or clearing the way for others to know and love You, too. Amen.

sermon  25

THEME

Each one of us is given special talents we must use.

BIBLE GEM

'There are different kinds of service, but the same Lord. There are different kinds of working, but in all of them and in everyone it is the same God at work.' *1 Corinthians 12:5, 6 (NIV)*

YOU WILL NEED

Some items from your bathroom cabinet, such as
• Shaving cream
• Hairspray
• Toothpaste in a pump
• Deodorant

ILLUSTRATION

Today I have brought some things from my bathroom cabinet – I'm sure you'll find similar items in yours. [Show them as you speak.] There is shaving foam: I always put it in the left corner of the top shelf; there's hairspray: I always put that in the right corner of the top shelf; there's toothpaste: I always put it in the left corner of the bottom shelf; and deodorant: I always put that in the right corner of the bottom shelf.

One of the days this week, I was in a great rush. I was running late! I had already put on my jacket, picked up my keys and then quickly dashed to the bathroom cabinet. I could hear the wind howling outside and I knew it was a day for hairspray! I closed my eyes, as I always do, because I don't want hairspray in my eyes; and reached to

the top shelf on the left for the canister. I sprayed and opened my
eyes! 'What on earth?' I yelled. I was covered in shaving foam, all fluffy
and white! [Covering your head with foam will add to the drama!]
Someone had switched the hairspray and shaving foam around, and I
hadn't noticed it because my eyes were closed! It took ages to clean up
and I had to change my jacket! I was late for my appointment. I felt so
silly!

I thought about the hairspray and the shaving foam a lot during that
day. It reminded me that God gave special talents to each of us. Just
like the hairspray's job is to help keep hair tidy and in place, and the
shaving foam is intended to help give a smooth shave, we each have
special talents to be used for God. The hairspray isn't any more
important than the shaving foam – they just have different functions. I
am not more important than anyone; I just have a particular work to do
for God that is probably different to the work He has asked you to do,
and you, and you. . . .

PRAYER

Dear God, thank You for showing me that any talents I
have do not make me more important than someone else
with different talents. Show me how to enjoy using my
talents for You and how to appreciate and value the talents of
others. Amen.

sermon  26

THEME

There are many pathways in life that do not end in happiness. The only path that leads to happiness is the one where Jesus takes the lead and walks beside us.

BIBLE GEM

'Jesus answered, "I am the way, and the truth, and the life. The only way to the Father is through me." ' *John 14:6 (NCV)*

YOU WILL NEED

Your passport

ILLUSTRATION

Do you like holidays? Did you go by plane, train, boat or car? Have you been on an overseas holiday?

I was about to go on an overseas holiday once. I was really looking forward to it. I was going to go to a very warm and sunny country when the weather where I lived was snowy and very grey. I had a good chat with the taxi driver on the way to the airport. He was very funny and made me laugh. It was a good way to start the holiday, I thought.

Once I was in the airport terminal I started checking in. I seemed to have everything I needed, except my passport! That was no good. There was no way I would be allowed to leave the country without one, and it was even less likely that the country I was going to would allow me to enter theirs.

Needless to say, I missed my flight. I had to take a taxi back home, and there it was, beside my bed, just where I had left it: my passport!

[Show them your passport.] Passports are very important documents and they hold a lot of detail. See, there is a photograph of me, my names, my date of birth, where I was born, my occupation. I have a special passport number. No one else has the same number. Even more important, the passport says I am a citizen of my country. The emblem of my country is on the front of my passport and I know the ambassadors of my country will do their best to protect me if anything goes wrong in the country I am visiting.

Jesus is like our passport to heaven. He has made me a citizen of heaven and promises to protect me and guard me while I am on this earth. Never lose sight of your heavenly passport. You'd be very disappointed if you missed out because you forgot to bring it with you!

PRAYER

Dear Jesus, thank You for being my passport to heaven where I will live forever with God one day. I promise to keep You in my heart always! Amen.

sermon (27)

THEME

We can spread happiness wherever we are.

BIBLE GEM

'Pleasant words are like a honeycomb, making people happy and healthy.' *Proverbs 16:24 (NCV)*

YOU WILL NEED

Some taster pots, some with a little honey in them and some others with lemon juice

ILLUSTRATION

When I was at school I was very unhappy when I was about nine years old. Unfortunately, my teacher had a very sharp tongue. She made the children feel stupid and the children didn't do well or make good progress. Her words were like this. . . . [Let some children take a little taste from the lemon taster pots. They will probably screw up their faces. Ask them why they screwed up their faces and talk about what it means to be a sour person and leave a sour taste in other people's mouths.] Miss Thompson was unfortunately like that – sour in her demeanour, sour with her words, and she created a sour atmosphere in the classroom.

After the first term, she took long leave for several months to go travelling around the world. We had a supply teacher. Mrs Dunn was just the opposite. She loved us. She smiled at us, spoke to us gently and encouraged us. We weren't frightened and anxious anymore, and we learned so much in those three months. We made very good progress. Mrs Dunn was like this. . . . [Get the same children to dip their fingers in the honey taster pots. They will probably go

'Mmmmm' and say it is sweet.] Mrs Dunn was like honey. She was as sweet as honey!

Our verse tells us that pleasant words are a honeycomb: they bring sweetness to ourselves and to others.

Jesus' words to the woman at the well were like honeycomb, too. They didn't make her feel bad about her life. They encouraged her to want to be like Jesus.

Determine to speak only pleasant, kind words – bring sweetness to all you do – you won't believe what a difference it will make to the atmosphere and to those around you!

PRAYER

Dear Jesus, I want my words to be like honeycomb – making people around me feel loved and special. May my words always be filled with sweetness. Amen.

sermon (28)

THEME

God uses us to spread His good news.

BIBLE GEM

'God uses us everywhere to spread His Word like a sweet-smelling perfume.' *2 Corinthians 2:15* *(author's paraphrase)*

YOU WILL NEED

- A sweet-smelling flower, like a rose, lily, frangipane, honeysuckle, jasmine, fragrant narcissus or any other highly perfumed flower
- Different perfume samples on tester strips from the perfume department
- A bottle of perfume you can spray

ILLUSTRATION

The flower I brought this morning is beautiful. [Talk about the colour, the shape of the flower and why you like it. It may have come from your garden – you could talk about how you take care of it.]

There is something more about this flower that I love. It has the most beautiful perfume. Would you like to smell it? [Give a few children a turn.]

Do you know perfumers extract these wonderful fragrances and mix them in different ways to make the hundreds of different types of perfumes people buy to spray on themselves to smell nice and feel good?

During the week, I visited the perfume department and asked if I could take a few tester strip samples for you to smell. [Let a few children smell a few and say which is the fragrance they like most.]

In our verse we learn that we are just like perfume [spray it into the air]. When we share God's love with others it spreads far and wide, much further than you can imagine, just like this sweet-smelling perfume!

PRAYER

Dear Jesus, I know how wonderful it is to smell the beautiful fragrance of the flowers in the garden. Help me to share Your word lovingly so the good news will spread like a sweet-smelling perfume, too. Amen.

sermon

THEME

Talents are to be used and developed: not hidden.

BIBLE GEM

'. . . people don't hide a light under a bowl. They put it on a lampstand so the light shines for all the people in the house.' *Matthew 5:15 (NCV)*

YOU WILL NEED

A small painting/print: don't let the children see the painting itself, just the back!

ILLUSTRATION

In the Bible we learn that God has given each one of us talents. It also teaches us that talents only grow and develop when we use them. When we don't use them, the talents don't develop and we may as well not have been given them in the first place.

Jesus used an example, comparing a talent to a light. If it is hidden under a wooden bowl the light is useless. When it is covered, the room is still in darkness. Just so with talents: when we hide them, they don't benefit anyone else.

A few weeks ago, I asked someone to paint my lounge walls. For the walls I chose a soft, pretty colour that was in a painting I was going to hang on the wall. The decorator was excited and he told me it would be a wonderful surprise when he had finished. I wasn't to enter the room until he had finished. He sealed the door with plastic sheets and worked hard, scraping, sanding and then painting.

Finally the job was done. He pulled down the plastic sheeting and told me to close my eyes as I entered the room. When he was ready, he told me to open them. I looked around the room. It looked wonderful! The walls were smooth and the colour was just right . . . but something was wrong. Where was the painting? It was there alright, but all I could see was the back of it [show the back of the painting]. The decorator had hung the painting back to front! There wasn't any picture. It looked awful.

That's just how it is when we hide our talents: no one can see the painting! We quickly turned the painting around. The picture was gorgeous, and it looked even more beautiful against the freshly painted wall.

When you are tempted to turn your 'painting to the wall' and hide your talent, remember, the picture looks so much better and should be hung in such a way that everyone can enjoy it!

PRAYER

Loving Jesus, thank You for giving me talents to bless others and to bring joy. Help me to know they will grow and develop the more I use them. Help me not to hide them through any laziness or shyness. Amen.

sermon ③⓪

THEME

Don't judge!

BIBLE GEM

'Don't judge others, or you will be judged. You will be judged in the same way that you judge others. . . .' *Matthew 7:1, 2 (NCV)*

YOU WILL NEED

- 2 bananas – one very ripe with black marks on the skin, and one without any marks on the skin (not quite ripe yet)
- Some small taster cubes of banana bread

ILLUSTRATION

I have two bananas here today [show the children the two bananas]. If I gave you one of them, which would you prefer? [Ask different children what they based their choice on – most are likely to say it is the not-quite-ripe one because it looks good.]

I think most/all of you chose the green/unripe banana because you liked the way it looked from the outside. Am I right? When we make judgements based just on what we see on the outside, we can make some big mistakes and we can come to very wrong conclusions. Jesus was very clear that we must not judge others.

I wanted to make a delicious banana loaf in the week. I used bananas that looked like the one with marks on it. Do you know why? The bananas that didn't look so good were actually the properly ripened ones. When they were peeled, the fruit inside was soft and sweet. The sugars in the fruit were fully developed and it would make the banana loaf really tasty and sweet. If I had used the bananas you like, they would not have mashed up into a nice smooth paste and the banana loaf would not have been nearly as delicious.

Let us remember that what we see on the outside doesn't always reveal what is on the inside. We may make judgements about people based on what we see on the outside, but we cannot see their hearts; we cannot read their minds. We never truly know enough about them to judge fairly. Only God can do that! From today, promise God, you will not judge anyone!

PRAYER

Dear Jesus, there are so many wonderful stories in the Bible where You have shown us why it is so wrong for us to judge others. Help us to accept each person we meet as one of Your children and to leave the judging to You. Amen.

sermon (31)

THEME

A positive attitude brings good health.

BIBLE GEM

'A happy heart is like good medicine. . . .'
Proverbs 17:22 (NCV)

YOU WILL NEED

A large flipchart piece of paper and a broad-tipped marker pen

ILLUSTRATION

Watch very carefully as I draw something on the paper. Don't say a word. Just be quiet and watch. . . .

[Draw a large square on the board, and then take a little time to think, and then draw a dot in the middle of the square. Select children and ask them what they can see in what you have drawn. Give opportunity to a few to speak.]

Did you notice, you talked about the black dot? That is what you noticed first and foremost. It claimed all your attention.

Now I want you to think about the space in the square around the dot. It was a huge space, much greater than the black dot, but you never even noticed it! It is the same with our lives: we often focus on the negative or bad things; we grumble about our friends, our homework, the chores we have to do at home, the little pocket money we get, the misunderstanding between friends. When you think about it, those little problems are really as small as the black dot in my drawing. They are tiny when we compare them to all the good things in life.

Stop looking at the black dots. Thank Jesus for your many

66

blessings and the exciting life you really enjoy! Be happy! The Bible says a positive attitude or a happy heart is just as good as a medicine. It can make sick people better!

PRAYER

Loving Father, I know how miserable I get when I just think negative thoughts. It does me no good. Help me always to find the positive in every situation and to be happy. Amen.

sermon 32

THEME

God should be our only treasure.

BIBLE GEM

'Don't store treasures for yourselves here on earth where moths and rust will destroy them. . . . But store your treasures in heaven where they cannot be destroyed by moths or rust. . . . Your heart will be where your treasure is.' *Matthew 6:19-21 (NCV)*

YOU WILL NEED

- A garment or piece of linen moths have eaten
- A variety of moth repellents: lavender, cedar balls, sticky strips, spray

ILLUSTRATION

I was so upset this week. I wanted to wear my favourite cashmere sweater because I was cold. It was a gift from a member of my family and for that reason it is particularly special to me. I like it because it is very thin, super soft and comfortable to wear. It always keeps me warm and toasty!

Moths are a real problem in the area where we live. Every autumn and spring I clear out all the clothes cupboards and check for evidence of moths in the clothes. If there is any, those clothes are thrown out immediately. I use a spray [like this one] to spray all the surfaces in the cupboards to repel the moths. All the clothes are washed again or sent to the dry cleaner and then they are packed neatly back on the shelves. Usually all the woollen things are put in mothproof bags like these. I spread cedar balls in the drawers and I put these moth-repellent strips on every shelf and hang them in the wardrobes. You would think, with all the care I take, that a moth wouldn't dare to enter my mothproof zone.

It is true that there are fewer now than when I first took very firm action to get rid of them, but the odd one still manages to make its way in somehow and do a bit of damage – like it did to this special sweater of mine!

Jesus told us that the possessions we love and cherish become our treasure. He warned that if 'things' become our treasure we will be disappointed, because they are quickly destroyed by things like moths or rust and they end up having no value at all. He reminded us that our friendship with Jesus should be our greatest treasure, because nothing can destroy that.

Think about the things that are so important to you that you couldn't bear to lose them . . . are they really worth it? Why not make Jesus your best treasure, and He will be yours forever!

PRAYER

Dear Jesus, I cannot think of anything more important to me than to be Your forever friend. Help me never to make anything else my treasure! Amen.

sermon  33

THEME

Understand the difference between a life filled with the Spirit and one that is not.

BIBLE GEM

'But the Spirit produces the fruit of love, joy, peace, patience, kindness, goodness, faithfulness, gentleness, self-control.' *Galatians 5:22, 23 (NCV)*

YOU WILL NEED

- A deflated football or basketball (any ball that needs to be pumped with air)
- A football pump

ILLUSTRATION

Who likes football/basketball? Could you play it without nets? (Yes, because you could use makeshift goals.) Could you play it without teammates? (Probably not the game, but you could practise kicking or dribbling.) Could you play it without a ball? (No!) I have a football here; would anyone like to have a little kick around with me? [Take out the ball and ask the children if they could play a game of football with it.] Why not? [Give a small kick and show them how useless the ball is.]

[Ask the children why the ball is useless.] It isn't pumped up. It needs to be filled with air. [Pull out the ball pump, and as you pump up the ball talk to the children about how much this reminds us of how we should be filled with the Holy Spirit.] The Holy Spirit in our lives is like the air in the ball. When the ball is filled with air, it can bounce, it can roll properly and children can play the game as it is meant to be played. [When the ball is filled with air, bounce it, and dribble it.] See how much better the ball is now that it is filled with air!

When we are not filled with the Holy Spirit, we hate more than we love, we are miserable more than we are happy, we argue and fight more than we are at peace, we are more impatient than we are patient, we are selfish more than we are kind, we do bad things more than we do good, we betray others more than we are loyal to them, we are rough more than we are gentle, and greedy more than we exercise self-control. We are just like the ball without air: not living as God intended. When we are filled with the Spirit, there is such a difference in who we are and the positive influence we have on others!

It's a no-brainer! Whoever would want to be like a sad, floppy ball? Ask the Holy Spirit to fill you entirely with everything that is good . . . and then just bounce with joy!

PRAYER

Holy Spirit, there is no way I want to be like a floppy, useless ball. Fill me with all Your goodness and help me to work with You for others. Amen.

sermon  34

THEME

Jesus is the 'water of life'.

BIBLE GEM

'Whoever drinks the water I give will never be thirsty. The water I give will become a spring of water gushing up inside that person, giving eternal life.' *John 4:14 (NCV)*

YOU WILL NEED

Two plants – one healthy and upright, the other droopy and in need of water

ILLUSTRATION

Has anyone here been really, really thirsty: so thirsty that they felt headachy and sick? It isn't good to be dehydrated. We need water for our brains to work properly. Without enough water, our brains are sluggish and slow and we find it hard to concentrate.

Animals and plants need water to survive and thrive. Look at this plant [show them the healthy one] – the leaves are firm and it looks upright and strong. I've checked it regularly and made sure it was watered regularly. Now look at this plant [show them the droopy plant]. Somehow I forgot about this plant and missed watering it. It is struggling and needs water soon, or it will die.

Jesus told us that He is like life-giving water; but, unlike the water we drink from the tap, we will never be spiritually thirsty when we drink the water of life. When we don't read His word, spend time with Him in prayer and give Him quiet time for Him to help us understand what He tells us, we will be just like the plant that is in trouble. We will be thirsty for everything He offers us.

When you drink water today, remind yourself to drink the water of life Jesus offers, too.

PRAYER

Dear Jesus, You are life-giving water to me. Thank You for quenching my thirst when I come to You. Amen.

sermon 35

THEME

Prayer is like oxygen to the Christian.

BIBLE GEM

'Pray continually, and give thanks whatever happens. That is what God wants for you in Christ Jesus.' *1 Thessalonians 5:17, 18 (NCV)*

YOU WILL NEED

- A tea light (candle)
- A clear glass to cover it
- Matches

ILLUSTRATION

Our Bible verse today tells us to pray all the time. Have you ever forgotten to pray? It is so easy to get on with things and forget to pray. It is so easy to struggle with problems and forget to ask God for ways to solve them. It is so easy to enjoy all the blessings of life and to forget to say 'Thank You' to God for being so good to us. There are many verses in the Bible that tell us how important prayer is. Jesus led by example. He prayed often for strength from God to do what He had to do. He prayed for the sick. He prayed for people who didn't truly know God. He prayed for those who were confused. Prayer was just as important to Him as breathing.

What would happen if you stopped breathing? You wouldn't be around for much longer would you?

In a way, this candle is just like us. It needs oxygen to burn. When all the oxygen is used, the flame goes out. Let me show you. [Light the candle and then put the glass over it. It will burn for a while.

Explain that there is oxygen trapped in the glass, but they should watch to see what will happen. Talk about prayer being like oxygen.] Prayer keeps us spiritually alive. When the flame goes out, we are just like that candle. When we forget to pray and neglect to spend time with God, the oxygen is used up, our candles burn out and we don't give any light.

Determine to be a candle whose flame never goes out!

PRAYER

Dear Jesus, thank You for showing me that prayer is as important to my life as the air I breathe. Only You can help me to keep my flame burning forever. Keep me burning brightly. . . . Amen.

sermon 36

THEME

Be slow to anger.

BIBLE GEM

'Do not become angry easily, because anger will not help you live the right kind of life God wants.'
James 1:19-20 (NCV)

YOU WILL NEED

- A few large balloons, not pumped
- A balloon pump

ILLUSTRATION

Do you get cross easily? Do you know anyone who loses their temper easily? Why do they get angry quickly? How do they show it?

The Bible tells us in a number of places that we need to exercise self-control. That means that, when we are annoyed or frustrated, we find better ways to deal with the problems, without resorting to angry outbursts.

[Start pumping the balloon.] Pretend you are this balloon. You get mad because you can't find your books and you need to leave the house right away to get to school on time; you get frustrated and you shout at your little sister. You blame her for moving the book (but she didn't). It just feels better to blame someone else! At school you are not chosen to be in the football team. You kick off, crying and screaming that it is unfair. You scream, 'It is so UNFAIR!' You get annoyed because the boy who lent you a pencil yesterday wants it back. He can't find his other pencil and the one you are using is the only one he has left. You cross your arms and sulk in your chair. 'How am I supposed to do my work now?' you huff and puff. You get your spelling test back and you say, 'I've had enough; the teacher thinks I can't spell!' and you explode with a horrible bang. [Pump until the balloon explodes.] Everyone you have been in contact with that day has suffered because you have not controlled your anger, and you have suffered even more!

If you haven't learned to manage your anger, speak to your parents and your teachers, and ask them to suggest ways you could try to control your temper.

There are stories about people in the Bible, too, whose anger was so out of control that they became violent. Can you think of someone in the Bible who got that angry? God wants something so much better for you, and that is why He has said to you, 'Be slow to anger.'

PRAYER

Dear Jesus, teach me to control my temper and never to get angry with anyone. Give me all the tools I need to manage every situation sensibly and calmly. Amen.

sermon  37

THEME

Don't be deceived!

BIBLE GEM

'**Be careful that you are not deceived, because many will come in My name, and say, "I AM"** . . . **don't follow them.**' *Luke 21:8 (author's translation)*

YOU WILL NEED

Make two small pies with a top pastry crust so they look identical. Put any pie filling in the bottom of one, and newspaper in the bottom of the other, so that it doesn't collapse. Glaze them and make them look as appetising as possible!

ILLUSTRATION

Yesterday I walked past the bakery and saw this amazing pie [it is the real pie]. It reminded me of the apple pies my grandmother used to make. It was so tempting, I decided to buy one. Then, as I walked a little further down the street, I thought it would be good to share the pie with friends today, so I quickly popped into the next baker's shop and saw a pie exactly the same as the pie in the first shop (well, almost exactly!). I bought that pie too. [Show the children the second pie. Ask them if they think it is the same.] I was told it was an apple pie, so I expect it will taste similar to the first pie. Do you think we should have a try and compare them? [Cut a slice out of the first pie. Put it on a plate and squirt some cream on it.] It looks good to eat!

Now ask the children again if they are sure it will be similar. Why do they think it will be? [Cut a slice and show them it is just a crust.]

What a disappointment! We've all been deceived! It turned out not to be what it said it was, or what we thought it was.

Jesus warned us that before He comes again there will be false teachers who will say amazing things and appear to be Jesus Himself. He warns us to look out for the signs, and not to be deceived as we have just been deceived! We will never know the difference unless we truly know God and understand His word to us in the Bible.

Stay close to Jesus. Be ready to meet Him, and don't be deceived!

PRAYER

Loving Father, thank You for warning us about false teachers. Keep us close to You so we will recognise them from a mile away. Help us to be ready each day for Your return. Amen.

sermon

THEME

We reap what we sow.

BIBLE GEM

'Do not be fooled: You cannot cheat God. People harvest only what they plant. If they plant to satisfy their sinful selves, their sinful selves will bring them ruin. But if they plant to please the Spirit, they will receive eternal life from the Spirit.' *Galatians 6:7-8 (NCV)*

YOU WILL NEED

- 2 or 3 packets of seed from the nursery
- A few seeds from a weed that grows in your area
- 4 paper plates

ILLUSTRATION

I bought some seeds this week because I want to grow some vegetables. I had prepared the soil a few weeks ago. I dug it up and broke up all the clumps, then I added loads of compost and dug that in. It is all settled and spongy now, ready for seeds.

[Show them the seeds – the packet says this is sweetcorn. Show them what the seed looks like on the plate.] When this grows and ripens what will I harvest? Are you sure it will be sweetcorn? Are you sure it won't be broccoli?

[Show them the seeds from the other packet – it says green beans. Show them what the seed looks like on another plate and compare them.] They look quite different. When this seed grows and ripens what will I harvest? Are you sure it will be beans? Are you sure it won't be courgettes?

Now look at these seeds – does anyone know what these are? They are dandelion seeds. They look quite different again. They are such a strong weed, they are almost impossible to get rid of in my garden. What would happen if I planted them with my corn and beans? Would they produce corn or beans? Why not? I'd be mad to plant them in my garden. I may as well give up planting any flowers or vegetables if I scattered them around, because I would have a garden of weeds!

Paul reminds us that if we live selfish lives we will harvest the fruit of selfishness; if we live lazy lives, we will harvest the consequences of that, too. Let's plant only good seed, the seed that God will harvest! I know what I want Jesus to harvest: I had better get planting!

PRAYER

Dear Jesus, thank You for reminding me to sow only good seed for the best harvest ever! Amen.

sermon (39)

THEME

Don't be trapped by sin.

BIBLE GEM

'If we confess our sins, he will forgive our sins. . . .
He will cleanse us from all the wrongs we have
done.' *1 John 1:9 (NCV)*

YOU WILL NEED

- A container that is not transparent, has tall sides and is just wide enough for a snug fit of your closed, empty fist
- A fistful of nuts inside the container

ILLUSTRATION

Sometimes we get into bad habits that can end in disappointment or disaster for us. Can you think of some of the things we do that separate us from Jesus? (Disobeying or ignoring our parents, taking things that don't belong to us, speaking badly of others, telling lies, treating some people with disrespect, failing to do our chores, not taking our learning seriously and wasting time, hanging out with those who are not a good influence on us. . . .)

Jason did all of those things. It started in small ways, at first, but he enjoyed it. He thought it made him look cool and gave him a sense of power. He had fooled himself. [Put in your hand and close it around the nuts.]

When things began to unravel, he started to feel bad. He was disappointed that he was dishonouring his parents, he felt bad that he included Jesus less and less in his life, and he wanted to change. He knew he needed to give up his bad habits, but he found it hard. Just like all these nuts in my hand that represent the bad habits we want to cling on to, Jason clung onto the bad stuff and wouldn't let go. While he held onto it, his hand was trapped in the container. He couldn't pull it out. [Show the children that it is impossible to free the hand while holding onto the nuts – ask them how it could affect day-to-day living.]

If only Jason knew that his hand wouldn't be trapped, if he just let go of the sin [release the nuts and slip out your hand] his hand would be free.

Do you have some bad habits, some secret sins you are holding onto? Perhaps this illustration has helped you to see how much they can affect your life, your happiness and your future. Why not let go of that ridiculous load of sin – allow Jesus to help you make good habits that will never trap you and limit you! Will you let go of those things today? Now?

PRAYER

Gracious Jesus, my hand is trapped because I'm holding onto some bad habits and sins. Make me brave enough to let go, and set me free of everything that separates me from You. Amen.

sermon  40

THEME

Don't gossip!

BIBLE GEM

'Speak no evil about anyone . . . live in peace, and . . . be gentle and polite to all people.' *Titus 3:2 (NCV)*

YOU WILL NEED

- A fairly large glass jar – put some sand or soil at the bottom; do it well in advance so the soil will settle and the water above it will be clear
- A big metal spoon and a teaspoon
- A hand-written note with these words: *"Today, I saw Joshua behaving strangely around your desk. The teacher assistant was in the classroom but had her back to him. When he saw me, he looked guilty and closed a plastic bag in his hand. If anything is missing from your desk, Joshua probably stole it! Pass this on (but don't let Miss or Joshua see it). – Dave"*

ILLUSTRATION

Have you heard anyone say, "He/she is a stirrer?" I have a big spoon here and I use it to stir the porridge for breakfast. I also have a teaspoon for stirring my hot drink. Big or small, they are both good for stirring. They are useful.

People who stir, though, are not helpful! They don't use spoons when they stir; instead, they say things to make a bad situation worse, or they say some things about people that are not true to turn others against them. Those people are called 'stirrers'.

Dave was a stirrer. He was in Joshua's class. I'm not sure why he wanted to turn his classmates against Joshua, but he did a thorough job of 'stirring' bad stuff one day.

[Pull out the note and read it.] Within hours, everyone, apart from the teacher and Joshua, 'knew' that Joshua was a thief and not to be trusted. As soon as his classmates got home, they shared the shocking news with their parents. Some parents who knew Joshua found it hard to believe. One of the mums rang Joshua's mum and said, 'I find it hard to believe. . . . You need to look into it.' Joshua's mum was upset. She decided to speak to Joshua's teacher first and take it from there.

The next day, Joshua was confused. Why were his classmates not talking to him? Why were they whispering behind their hands so he couldn't hear? Why did they not include him in their games anymore?

Later in the day, when Joshua left the class for his piano lesson, the teacher gathered the children round her on the carpet. She was pale, as though she had had a big shock! She took a jar of water like this and started to talk to the children. [Take the jar of water and demonstrate as you continue the story.] 'You know, someone in our classroom has been stirring.' She took the big spoon and stirred. [Talk about how the water changes.] 'This is what happens when people stir. This morning I learned that you had read a note that said Joshua was a thief. That note stirred trouble. It wasn't true. Joshua wasn't stealing from your desks. Did each of you find a surprise cookie in your desks yesterday? When Joshua asked me if he could put a surprise cookie in each of your desks I said he could. Not one of you guessed who had put it there!' The teacher stirred the muddy water again and said, 'It is wrong to gossip. Someone in this class jumped to conclusions; they didn't know the whole story, and they made one up and spread a horrible lie.' The children were sad that they had been caught in the trail of gossip. One by one they said they were sorry.

'From today, be clear, there is no place for gossip!' the teacher said firmly. 'We will not speak evil of anyone!' And the class responded together, 'We will speak no evil of anyone!'

PRAYER

Dear Jesus, help me to speak only good of others and never to spread gossip! Amen.

sermon 41

THEME

Magnify God in your life!

BIBLE GEM

'My soul magnifies the Lord. . . .' *Luke 1:46 (ESV)*

YOU WILL NEED

- Two bottles that look the same, with very fine/small print on the directions (for example, shampoo and hair conditioner bottles)
- A magnifying glass

ILLUSTRATION

I can't see very well without my glasses. When I don't wear them, the letters in a book are so tiny, I cannot make out what they are. You can imagine, it is even worse when I try to read writing when the font is tiny!

When I am in the shower and I wash my hair the bottles look the same [show the bottles]. The only difference is that one has shampoo in it and the other has conditioner in it. So many times I have poured conditioner into my hand, when I needed to wash my hair with shampoo first. The conditioner in my hand is wasted and then washed away down the drain. To solve the problem, I now have a magnifying glass that magnifies the letters – they are really large and I can read them, even without my glasses. I have started taking it with me when I go shopping so I can read the ingredient list on the back of food packages, to make sure they are all healthy.

When we magnify the Lord by the way we live, people are able to read God's character. What words do you think they might read when we magnify God? [Get children to make suggestions.]

Will you be a magnifier for God? Will you help others to see Him clearly so they will know how much He loves them?

PRAYER

Dear Father God, just as Jesus magnified Your character when He lived on earth, help us to magnify You, too. Amen.

sermon (42)

THEME

God protects me in the storms.

BIBLE GEM

'This covering . . . will provide a safe place to hide from the storm and rain.' *Isaiah 4:6 (NCV)*

YOU WILL NEED

- A set of very dripping-wet clothes in a bowl
- A rope tied to anything that can float – any swimming aid, or an empty two-litre plastic bottle with the cap firmly screwed on

ILLUSTRATION

Do you see these wet clothes? How do you think they came to be dripping wet? [Hold them up and show the children how wet they are.] You could be mistaken for thinking they were washed and we forgot to hang them out to dry. . . . There's a real story attached to these soggy, wet, dripping clothes, and it happened to me!

I was wearing these clothes when I went for a boat ride with my friend. The weather seemed fine and the water was still. We believed we were safe. We were chatting and enjoying being together, and we didn't notice the little changes that come before a storm, and then it seemed, without warning, that a huge wind swept in the biggest clouds that opened just above our boat. We started rowing furiously to get to the shore; but the harder we rowed, the more it seemed we were rowing in glue that wouldn't let us move to the shore. My friend was tired. He stopped for just a short moment and the oar bounced away out of our reach. We decided to swim back to the shore, but someone walking his dog out there noticed we were in trouble. 'I'll get help,' he shouted to us; 'hang in there!' We had no idea what kind of help he had in mind.

It seemed like an age, but it wasn't very long. He had dashed to his car and picked up a rope and a large, empty plastic bottle. As he ran towards the shore, he knotted the rope to the plastic and made a makeshift float. He swung his arm out wide and hurled his makeshift lifeline to me and my friend. My friend went first, because he was the weaker swimmer. He held onto the plastic bottle and kicked for all he was worth as the life-saver on the other side pulled in the rope. When my friend was safely on the shore, he did the same for me. We were exhausted. Our hearts were pounding with fear, but we hugged that man as if we had known him all our lives. He had saved us – and, if my wet clothes here could speak, they would tell you the story, too.

My friend's little boat is probably stranded far from where it should be. I hope it wasn't wrecked. But the good part of the story was that a kind man rescued us and we are safe.

I've thought a lot about that man, the makeshift lifebelt and my wet clothes in the last few hours. It reminded me of how it is in life for all of us. The sea, like life, is calm and fine for most of the time, but when the storms come – the disappointments, the hard bits about life – we really can't cope with them very well without a life-saver. When you are faced with the hard bits of life, the bits that don't make sense, remember to call on Jesus to be your life-saver. . . . I am so glad Jesus is my life-saver. He didn't just throw out a makeshift life-belt to save me . . . He gave his own life so I can be with Him for all eternity.

And you know . . . He has done the same for you and everyone in the whole wide world!

PRAYER

Dear Jesus, sometimes we get into difficulty because that is just how life is. Thank You for saving us from discouragement and despair, and helping us through the hard bits. Other times we get into difficulty through our own stupidity and the foolish decisions we make. Even then You have promised to help us work our way out of these tricky situations. Thank You for being my life-saver – not just for now, but forever. Amen.

sermon 43

THEME

Hard hearts aren't as good as soft hearts.

BIBLE GEM

'Do not harden your hearts [against God].'
Hebrews 3:8 (NKJV)

YOU WILL NEED

- Two mixing bowls
- Ingredients for a cake: 1 cup of flour, some baking powder, sugar, a little oil, vanilla, or chocolate powder
- Another empty bowl
- A wooden spoon
- Two boiled eggs

ILLUSTRATION

How many of you like cake? What is your favourite cake? Have any of you helped to bake a cake yet?

What are the ingredients you need to bake a cake? [Get children to respond and repeat.]

[Tell the children you want to mix a cake quickly as you speak to them. Tell the children what is in the dry ingredient mix in one bowl and give it a little stir. You could ask one or two children to give it a stir as well. Then tell them that you have to beat the eggs until they are fluffy and foamy before you add the dry ingredients. Be dramatic about cracking open the eggs – they don't crack as they normally do. Are they just being difficult? Start smashing the shell, and, once shelled, show the children the hard-boiled egg. Ask them if that is how the eggs should be to make a cake.]

There, at last, the shells are off the eggs. [Put them in the bowl and start whisking.] Something is very wrong here. [Ask the children why the eggs are not whisking. Put the eggs into the flour mixture and show the children what it looks like. Ask them if that is what their mother's cake batter looks like before she puts it in the oven.] What is wrong with it? [Establish that there is a problem with the eggs.]

Ah, we cannot make a cake as we know it with boiled eggs, can we? When they are boiled they go solid and they cannot mix with the other ingredients anymore. To make a cake we need eggs to be runny and smooth. This makes them bring the whole mixture together to turn it into something new – a batter that will become a delicious cake! Sadly, these solid eggs are no good.

In our verse, Paul warned his friends not to harden their hearts against God. When things go wrong, it isn't God's fault. We don't blame Him and say He doesn't care and turn our backs on Him. If we do, our hearts harden like the boiled egg, and the egg cannot be used for the many different uses there are for fresh eggs. Hardened eggs cannot change back to runny eggs. They can only ever be hard-boiled eggs! Just so with hardened hearts: we cannot do all the amazing things God planned for us to do for Him.

Draw near to God. Keep your hearts in perfect shape for Him!

PRAYER

Dear Jesus, You have the gentlest heart of love for everyone, and that is just the kind of heart I want. Keep me from developing a hardened heart that cannot bring peace, love and happiness to everyone. Amen.

sermon 44

THEME

Teamwork and encouragement go together.

BIBLE GEM

'For the body is not one member, but many.'
1 Corinthians 12:14 (KJV)

YOU WILL NEED

A tub that can hold a set of wax crayons or felt-tip pens
upright with a snug fit

ILLUSTRATION

You come to church every week. If someone asks you, 'What is
church?' what goes through your mind first? Is it the building? Is it the
pastor? Do you think of the deacons and deaconesses? The organist?
The choir? The sermon? The members?

In our verse today, Paul explains that the church – and he calls the
church the body of Jesus – isn't just the pastor, or just one important
person. He says that the church is a big team of lots of people, and
each has an important part to play in making the team work well
together.

Look at the crayons – when I used them a few minutes ago, they
were flopping all over the place. Let me show you. [Try and make
them stand upright by pulling them all together in your hands and
letting go.] That wasn't a great success, was it? Let's try something
else. [Just put a few in the tub so they fall at an angle and then pile
the rest on top – you won't be able to fit them all in this way. Some
will fall out and you'll have great difficulty trying to reach the crayons
right at the bottom. Talk about how it looks like some crayons want

the best spot/jobs in the church, but they are so far down in the tub that no one can reach them when they need their help!]

[Finally, draw up all the crayons neatly in both hands and guide them all together into the tub.] They all fit in; they are standing like tall soldiers; all the crayons around them are standing tall, supporting one another. And, best of all, the person who wants to use them can reach them all easily. [Suggest that the tub is Jesus, who keeps them all together so none of the crayons fall out.]

Churches where everyone works together as a team are happy places, where the members grow and the church grows. Churches where people are only interested in being powerful, rather than being an influence for good, are places where there are lots of squabbles, lots of sadness and unhappiness.

Determine today that you will always be a good team player in your church. Support your friends, your parents, your teachers, your pastor and everyone who helps to make everything run smoothly. God will bless our church and make it grow. . . .

PRAYER

Dear Jesus, You are a good team player and I want to be part of Your team. Give me the right attitude to always encourage, help and support my friends at church. Amen.

sermon

THEME

Whatever is inside spills out when you are squeezed.

BIBLE GEM

'For as he thinks within himself, so he is.'
Proverbs 23:7 (ISV)

YOU WILL NEED

- A bowl with deep sides and a bottle of clean water
- Two sponges – cellulose sponges are ideal
- Make sure both sponges are damp, and soak one either in water that is coloured with food colouring, or muddy water; the second sponge should only be soaked in clean water
- Place each sponge on an individual plate for the children to see

ILLUSTRATION

Today we have two sponges here. Do you know what is so good about sponges? They are good for soaking up water or other liquids. When we have a spill in the kitchen, sponges are the best and quickest way to mop it all away. The other good thing about them is it is so easy to squeeze the water out of them when the job is done.

Sponges remind me of the verse in the Bible that tells us that our thoughts shape the kind of people we are. We are like sponges; we soak up so much of everything that is around us. We can soak up good things, but very often we seem to soak up the messy, ugly stuff more. Can we think about the good things that are good for us to soak up? [Let the children suggest a few behaviours and attitudes.] Now tell me some of the bad influences that are so easy to soak up. [Again, let the children suggest a few.]

Mostly, we cannot tell what is on the inside of a person: but, when the tough times come, what comes out of our mouths tells us what is going on in the heart. Sarah may speak only good things when all is going well, but what comes out of her mouth when the bad times come? [Squeeze the dirty sponge and show the children how dirty the water is.] Gossip, swear words, lies, everything that does not come from God! Someone else – Daniel, for instance – may seem a little rough, but what comes out of his mouth when the tough times come? [Squeeze the sponge with the clean water and show the children how clean it is.] He prays and asks God to help him solve the problems; he reminds others that God is with him; he chooses not be afraid. He tells the truth, and he will only speak well of others. . . .'

If you were a sponge right now, and your friend squeezed you, what kind of water would your friend squeeze out of you? Clean? Dirty? Most of us have a little dirt we need to ask Jesus to wash away. [Now pour the clean water from the bottle fairly slowly over the dirty sponge as you wash away the dirt, and the water starts to run clean. Show the children how clean the water is when you squeeze the sponge.]

PRAYER

Dear Jesus, keep my thoughts pure; protect me from the bad influences all around me that can fill my mind so easily. When I do absorb some of the dirt, wash me clean again: in Jesus' name, amen.

sermon 46

THEME

God protects me and saves me.

BIBLE GEM

'The LORD is my rock, my fortress and my deliverer. . . .' *Psalm 18:2 (NIV)*

YOU WILL NEED

Two or three interesting stones

ILLUSTRATION

[Tell the children you have some interesting stones to show them. Let some of them feel them and describe them to the rest of the group.]

Stones can be interesting in many ways. Some, like diamonds and rubies, are valuable and expensive. People buy them mostly for adornment. Other rocks, like marble, are used in beautiful buildings. Sandstone is used to build large, important buildings because stonemasons can carve ornate features on them.

Have you noticed how important rocks and stones are when you climb a steep hill or mountain? We usually look for the rocks that are firm and secure in the earth, because they will hold our weight and we are less likely to slip and fall. In some places, people have painted the secure rocks in red for the climbers. They aren't always the biggest or most beautiful rocks. If you didn't know that they had been identified as safe, you wouldn't even give them a second look. Their most important feature is that they are securely embedded in the mountainside.

The psalmist reminds us that Jesus is our Rock. In the hard times, He is like the secure rock we can rely on to help us reach the top of the mountain. He is strong; He protects us and keeps us safe.

PRAYER

Dear Jesus, thank You for being my Rock. Help me to always depend on You. Amen.

sermon 47

BIBLE GEM

'Here I am! I stand at the door and knock. If you hear my voice and open the door, I will come in. . . .' *Revelation 3:20 (NCV)*

YOU WILL NEED

A collection of different keys – big, old, house, car, shed, treasure box or cash box – and a padlock

ILLUSTRATION

[Show the children your collection of keys. Ask them if they can guess what the different keys might be used for. Ask one of the children to try to open a padlock with the biggest key. Talk about why it didn't work. Let them guess which key would open the padlock and try it. When the padlock is finally opened, apply the illustration.]

We have keys to lock our homes, our cars and anything we value, because we want to keep them safe. Did you notice that we didn't have a key that could unlock the house, the car and the padlock? Each lock had its own key.

We have been given keys to our hearts, too. They don't look like these, but they are our own free will. Jesus knocks at the door of our hearts, politely and gently. When we open our hearts to Him, what a difference He makes in our lives! Remember, keys are not only for locking, but for unlocking, too. . . . Why not use your key to open the door of your heart to Jesus today?

PRAYER

Dear Jesus, thank You for giving me the key to my heart. I open my heart to You today. Help me to open it to You every day. Amen.

sermon 48

THEME

Are you who you say you are, or are you a pretend Christian?

BIBLE GEM

'Therefore by their fruits you will know them.'
Matthew 7:20 (NJKV)

YOU WILL NEED

- A bottle of fragrant perfume or a diffuser bottle with lovely fragrant contents
- An empty perfume bottle or diffuser bottle (make sure this bottle is washed well so that there is no hint of the original contents): put something that doesn't smell good inside the bottle – for example, the liquid from a rotten onion or potato; if you can't find these, buy a little very strong awful-smelling cheese

ILLUSTRATION

Have you heard some grown-ups say, 'It does what it says on the tin'? When they say that, they mean that the item they have bought and use lives up to the claims of the makers and sellers. If it is a vacuum cleaner – it is a good one and it works well. If it is a computer – it has all the features you expected when you bought it.

Perfumes or room fragrances are like that, too. I have one here that I have at my front door – it always smells wonderful when you open the door and you enter the house. I hope it makes my guests feel welcome and special when they smell it. [Give the children opportunity to smell it.]

Here I have another bottle of room fragrance. Did you see? It looks just like the other one. It has the same label on the front and it has the same name. Now take a little sniff of it. . . . [Get the children to smell it as you hold it under their noses.]

Did it smell the same as the fragrance in the first bottle? You expected it to, didn't you? Why did you expect it to? [Talk about the same bottle, label and name.] This was just the foulest-smelling concoction in a bottle, wasn't it? It definitely did not do what it says on the tin, did it?

As young Christians we need to take care that we represent Jesus well. We also need to be who we say we are on the tin.

Jesus told a story once about people who were not what they said they were on the tin. He called them hypocrites! They were critical of everyone else and thought they were above everyone else, but inside the bottle was the vilest-smelling liquid ever. Jesus said they were like white sepulchres: impressive on the outside, but filled with rotting bones.

Determine today that you will be true to Jesus – when people get to know you, they will always say, 'That boy/that girl is who they say they are on the tin!'

PRAYER

Dear Jesus, I can only be who I say I am on the tin when I place my life in Your hands and allow Your love to shine through. Help me to be who I say I am on the tin. Amen.

sermon 49

THEME

We can have forgiveness and a fresh start.

BIBLE GEM

'Create in me a clean heart, O God. . . .'
Psalm 51:10 (NKJV)

YOU WILL NEED

- A tarnished piece of silverware or brassware
- Silver cleaner or Brasso and polishing cloths
- Gloves

ILLUSTRATION

We have a few pieces of silver in our house that have been passed down through the family. They are very beautiful, but take a lot of work to keep sparkling and at their best. It takes a lot of time to get through them all, and a lot of rubbing and polishing!

This week, I started cleaning some of the pieces for us to use over the Christmas season. It took several hours, and I had just one or two more pieces to polish. I brought one piece with me to show just how bad and ugly it looks. [Show them the piece. Ask the children: if they saw it looking like that in a shop, would they buy it?] Most of us wouldn't give it a second look. We'd think it was a piece of old rubbish. [Get the children to describe what it looks like.]

Do you know, that is exactly how we all are – we judge things by what they look like on the outside. You are right: it doesn't look good. If someone told you it was valuable, would you change your mind? Would you suddenly find something about it that was beautiful?

The Bible tells us that Jesus doesn't look on the outside. He knows the value of each human being, because He paid the price for each one of us when He died on the cross.

[Put on your gloves and start applying the polish to the object. Ask the children if it looks any better. The object will look a little different, though not better.] That is not a problem to God. He says, 'My work with you isn't finished yet . . . I'm still polishing you, and you will be seen in the best possible way.' [Keep rubbing, and allow the polish to dry for a minute or so as you ask the children what you think Jesus will polish away from our lives, like the tarnish on the silver. Take a soft polishing cloth to start bringing up the shine. Ask the children if it looks better. Ask them, if they were polishing, would they stop now? Is the job good enough? Some may say yes, but tell them God keeps on working on your life, polishing away, and finally . . . hold up the object, gleaming and bright! Ask them again: if they saw the object in the shop, would they think it was pretty enough to buy?]

We are just like that piece of silver with ugly tarnish, simply caused by the environment around us. God sees what we can truly be like, and, when we give our hearts to Him, He begins His work of polishing us for His glory.

Thank God for never thinking you are worthless or too tarnished to polish. Thank Him for the good job He is doing of polishing every stain out of every little corner of your life!

PRAYER

Dear God, just as You heard David's prayer, hear mine. . . . Make my heart pure, O God. Amen.

sermon (50)

THEME

Half the battle is won with a positive attitude.

BIBLE GEM

'All things work together for good to those who love God. . . .' *Romans 8:28 (NKJV)*

YOU WILL NEED

A bottle of bubble solution, or a bubble gun (if you can find a large bubble wand you can blow a variety of different-sized bubbles)

ILLUSTRATION

Bubbles are great fun, aren't they? They are so airy and light, and when the light catches them you can see the beautiful colours of the rainbow in their surfaces.

When I was young we used to sing a song called, 'You can Smile . . .'. It was a cheerful, happy song, and we liked singing it. The words to the first verse went something like this:

'There are many troubles that will burst like bubbles

There are many shadows that will disappear

When you learn to meet them, with a smile to greet them,

For a smile is better than a frown or tear.

You can smile, when you can't say a word, you can smile

When it's cloudy or fair, you can smile anytime, anywhere!'

Do any of you know why bubbles burst so easily? It is interesting: the longer a bubble floats in the air, the thinner the surface of the bubble gets, and eventually it cannot resist the pressure in the air, and it bursts.

The next time you are discouraged, or you are worried about anything, think of the problem as just a little bubble floating in the air: it won't be long before your positive attitude and happy disposition force so much pressure on it that it will pop and disappear.

Scientists have found that people who don't give up, who find something positive in every situation and keep on smiling and sharing their happiness, are a lot more successful, despite any problems that come their way. That is a good enough reason to be cheerful and positive, don't you think?

PRAYER

Dear Father God, help me to see everything that troubles me as a bubble that will soon pop and disappear. There is so much to make me happy. Help me never to forget that. Amen.

sermon (51)

THEME

The more you give away God's love, the more you receive – it never runs out!

BIBLE GEM

'Have you ever come on anything quite like this extravagant generosity of God . . . ?'
Romans 11:33 (MSG)

YOU WILL NEED

- A large sheet of flipchart paper with large words written in felt-tip: GOD'S LOVE
- A pair of scissors

ILLUSTRATION

Do you like sharing? Giving away your toys? Your sweets? Sometimes it is really hard. I remember one Christmas when I received two beautiful dolls. My aunt had just visited Wales and she brought me a beautiful Welsh doll. I loved her hat and her little shawl. My mum explained there was a little girl in my church who wasn't going to have a nice Christmas, and asked if it wouldn't be nice to make her Christmas special by giving her one of my dolls. I agreed, but when it came to choosing it was so hard. My mum asked me which was my favourite. 'The Welsh doll,' I said, immediately. 'That's it,' she said. 'Give the little girl "the Welsh doll".' (I still don't know who the little girl was, because the family wanted my mum to keep her knowledge of the family's hardship private. I know the little girl received the doll because her parents wrote me a little note.)

I had one less doll in my toy box, and I'm ashamed to say, I missed her!

God's love isn't like that, though. It is a very strange thing: the more you give away God's love, the more there is to give away.

Let's say this large sheet of paper represents God's love. How many corners are there on the paper? [4] If I cut off one of the corners and I give it to [one of the children], how many corners do we have all together now? [5 on the big sheet and 3 in the child's hand – 8] Let's count them. If I cut another corner and share it with you, how many corners do we have altogether? [12] . . . and the next corner? [16] . . . and the fourth corner? [20] – we can keep cutting off the corners, until it isn't a rectangular shape anymore, but a circle – isn't that wonderful? God's love encircling us.

It is so true: the more of God's love we give away, the bigger it gets.

God is generous with His love, His forgiveness. As His children, He reminds us that, like the widow's oil that she shared with Elijah, the more we share His love, the more we have to give away!

PRAYER

Dear Father, Your love is so amazing – it just grows and grows the more we share it. I want to share it with everyone I know. . . . Amen.

sermon

THEME

Make some new year's promises to God.

BIBLE GEM

'The Lord's mercies . . . are new every morning: great is thy faithfulness.' *Lamentations 3:22, 23 (KJV)*

YOU WILL NEED

A new, unused notebook with a beautiful cover and crisp, clean white pages inside

ILLUSTRATION

The old year is almost past and we will shortly start a brand-new year. I like brand-new years. It's a time when many people make changes to their lives; they resolve to give up bad habits and form new good habits. It is such a positive time of the year!

[Show a notebook you have used in the past year.] Do you see this notebook? I've written lots of things in it this past year. [Mention some of the things.] Sometimes I have written neatly; other times it has been a bit scruffy because I have been sitting in an awkward position or I've been in a hurry. I've written with pens of different colours and with pencils, and I've stuck in some sticky notes. But the book is filled now. It is a book about a year that is over. It is history!

[Show the new book.] This is the notebook I shall use in the coming year. The cover is beautiful, the corners are clean and neat, and the pages inside are crisp, pure white and waiting for me to fill them with writing. . . . I have no idea what I will write on those pages, but I am excited to find out what it will be.

Our lives are like this new notebook in the coming year: all kinds of opportunities and exciting things are waiting to fill its pages. If you were planning to write the story of your life in the coming year, what would you like people to read about you, if they picked it up and started reading? Would it be beautiful, pure, honest and good? [Let the children respond.]

It can be . . . and I am sure it will, if you allow Jesus to guide your pen! Happy New Year to all!

PRAYER

Dear Jesus, there is an exciting new year ahead – I know I can look forward to it if we enter the new year together. May the story in my new book be one that You will help me to write, Jesus. Thank You! Amen.

UNFORGETTABLE STORIES

20 STORIES FOR TEACHING CHILDREN VALUES

Help teach your children to understand and develop values like friendship, courage, and patience.

Each story in this collection covers an important life value, starting off with the Word of God, and finishing with questions to think about in their own lives, plus a prayer to lead them into a deeper relationship with God.

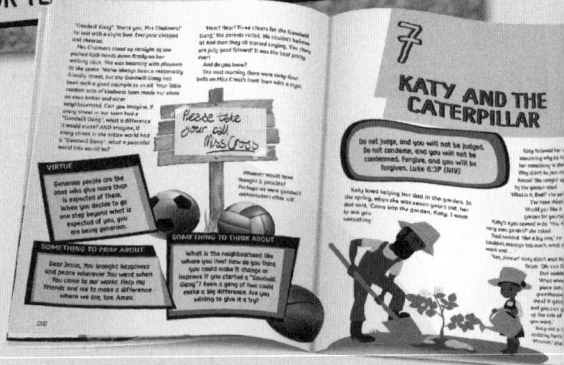

A topsy-turvy children's book, beautifully illustrated, telling the story of Ben – whose attitude of forgiveness and inclusion turned around the lives of his friends – and Wendy, who learned to hand over her care and worries to God.

Autumn House